# BESIDE THE STILL WATERS

†

# BESIDE THE STILL WATERS

An Illustrated Bible Anthology

SELECTED AND WITH AN INTRODUCTION BY
JAMES BENTLEY

BROCKHAMPTON PRESS
LONDON

†

PUBLISHED IN 1993 BY AURUM PRESS LTD,
25 BEDFORD AVENUE, LONDON WC1B 3AT

A catalogue record for this book is available from the British Library

ISBN 1-86019-925-9

10  9  8  7 6  5  4 3  2  1

1997 1996 1995 1994 1993

Opposite title page: VELÁZQUEZ (1599–1660), *CRUCIFIXION* (DETAIL)

Designed by Sasha Kennedy/ACE Limited

**Printed in Dubai by Oriental Press**

This edition published 1999 by Brockhampton Press,
a member of Hodder Headline PLC Group

✝

# CONTENTS

✝

## LOVE 99

# Acknowledgements

Extracts from the Authorised Version of the Bible (The King James Bible), the rights of which are vested in the Crown, are reproduced by permission of the Crown's Patentee, Cambridge University Press.

The illustrations were supplied by the Bridgeman Art Library, 19 Chepstow Road, London W2 5BP.

The publishers wish to thank the following for permission to reproduce the pictures:

Bibliothèque Nationale, Paris/Giraudon pp.85, 98, 105

Birmingham City Museums & Art Gallery p.109

Bonhams, London pp.70, 86

British Library, London pp.57, 66

British Museum, London p.17

Christie's, London pp.14, 21, 26, 53

Collegio Alberoni, Piacenza p.25

Denis Mahon Collection p.45

Eglise Ste. Marie Madeleine, Aix en Provence/Giraudon p.78

Forbes Magazine Collection, New York p.110

Galleria degli Uffizi, Florence p.81

Gemaldegalerie, Dresden p.121

Johnny van Haeften Gallery, London pp.54, 61, 101

Kress Collection, Washington DC p.33

Kunsthistorisches Museum, Vienna p.97

Louvre, Paris/Giraudon p.113

Louvre, Paris/Lauros-Giraudon p.117

Musèe Departemental des Vosges, France p.22

Musèe des Beaux-Arts, Rouen p.58

Musèe des Beaux-Arts, Rouen/Giraudon pp.90, 94

Musée des Beaux-Arts, Nantes/Giraudon pp.34, 46

Museo di San Marco dell'Angelico, Florence p.29

Museo Diocesano, Lerida, Catalunya/Index p.69

Muzeum Narodowe, Warsaw p.18

National Gallery, London p.106

National Gallery of Scotland, Edinburgh p.118

Osterreichische Nationalbibliothek, Vienna p.82

Phillips, The International Fine Art Auctioneers pp.73, 74

Prado, Madrid/Index opposite title page, p.38

Prado, Madrid pp.41, 42, 50, 89, 114

Private Collection p.93

Pushkin Museum, Moscow p.125

Royal Chapel, Grenada p.37

Sotheby's, London p.62

Stedelijk Museum "De Lakenhal", Leiden p.102

Unterlinden Museum, Colmar, France p.77

By courtesy of the Board of Trustees of the V & A p.122

Vatican Library, Rome p.65

Werner Collection, Luton Hoo, Bedfordshire p.49

York City Art Gallery p.30

# INTRODUCTION

The most majestic version of the Bible in English, from which all the following extracts are taken, was made possible by a fifteenth-century battle and a fifteenth-century invention.

Some battles transform society in unexpected ways. In May 1453 the Turks stormed Constantinople. Countless scholars fled to Europe. They found refuge amongst other scholars who longed to learn from them the Greek language which for centuries had been virtually lost to the western world. And Greek was the original language of the Christian gospels.

Three years after the fall of Constantinople the newly invented printing presses issued their first book. It was an edition of the Bible, printed at Mainz by Johann Gutenberg. Gutenberg's Bible was published in Latin; but the new learning from Constantinople and the printing presses set the stage for scholars not only to translate the Holy Scriptures from their original Greek and Hebrew but also to disseminate them far and wide amongst ordinary people.

In consequence the following two centuries were the golden age of Bible translation. First the Protestant reformer Martin Luther produced a magnificent German version of the Scriptures. In England William Tyndale began translating the New Testament from the Greek in 1523. Strangely, as it now seems, the church authorities found Tyndale's project threatening, and Tyndale fled abroad in 1524, never returning to Britain. He produced translations of the whole Bible from Greek and Hebrew, having them secretly printed at Worms, but his enemies pursued him and in 1536 he was caught, strangled and burnt at the stake. His last words were, 'Lord, open the king of England's eyes.'

Oddly enough, the king's eyes were at least half open. Henry VIII had already commissioned an English translation of the Bible. As the sixteenth century progressed, further translations proliferated. So did religious strife, and when James VI of Scotland became James I of England in 1603, he called a conference at Hampton Court to try to bring about a measure of religious peace. There one divine, Dr John Reynolds, suggested that the king might authorize a new English version of the Bible. King James agreed.

Six companies of scholars, two meeting at Oxford, two at Cambridge and two at Westminster, toiled over the new version.

They utilized parts of most of the previous English translations. 'Truly we never thought to make a new translation, nor yet to make of a bad one a good one, but to make a good one better, or out of many good ones one principal good one', they declared. They succeeded, producing an unrivalled literary and religious masterpiece.

The translation authorized by King James was published in 1611. William Shakespeare was still alive, and this was the greatest age of English prose and poetry. All subsequent revisions have acknowledged the music of this 1611 Bible, 'its cadences, and the felicities of its rhythm', as the revisers of 1881 put it, 'its simplicity, its dignity, its power, its happy turns of expression'.

In 1896 the distinguished scholar Frederic G. Kenyon attempted to sum up its influence. He commented that 'great as has been the literary significance of the Authorised Version, its religious significance has been greater still'. He continued: 'For nearly three centuries it has been the Bible, not merely of public use, not merely of one sect or party, not even of a single country, but of the whole nation and of every English-speaking country on the face of the globe. It has been the literature of millions who have read little else, it has been the guide of conduct to men and women of every class in life and of every rank in learning and education.' Kenyon concluded that this Bible 'was a national work in its creation, and it has been a national treasure since its completion'.

What makes the Bible unique, whether in English or in its original tongues? Obviously insight into the human condition is part of its spell, insight which moreover comes for the most part from stories rather than a succession of moral statements. Great stories are imbued with multiple meanings.

Often in these biblical tales, men and women who lived over 2000 years ago challenge us to interpret their insights in our own ways. The Jewish prophet Elijah, for example, promised a vision of God, sees first an earthquake. The Bible declares, 'but the Lord was not in the earthquake', adding that after the earthquake came a fire – 'but the Lord was not in the fire: and after the fire, a still, small voice'. What is this still small voice, and why is a still, small voice superior to earthquake and fire? We are challenged to ponder the question ourselves.

The Bible is about faith; but its authors knew that it is difficult to believe. In one of the stories printed here, Jesus promises to heal a man's deaf and dumb child. The father longs to believe that this can happen, but what he cries, with tears, is the arresting paradox, 'Lord, I believe; help thou mine unbelief.'

The stories I have selected almost invariably have a religious moral attached to them; but again and again the seductiveness of tale itself overwhelms the moral. Take the account of how Joseph refuses to be seduced by the wife of his master Potiphar. Its lesson is that 'the Lord was with Joseph, and shewed him mercy'. But what sticks in one's mind is the story rather than the lesson.

When Ezekiel sees a valley of skeletons come to life again, this is set out as an image of how God will bring new life to the downtrodden children of Israel. But again the image of the valley of dry bones seems more potent than the moral. And the same is true with the tale of how David seduced a married woman named Bathsheba and had her husband killed. This time, however, the doom-laden final sentence of this chapter in the Bible is ominous: 'But the thing that David had done displeased the Lord.' Morality, it is implied, cannot be mocked.

Apart from imparting such age-old insights, the King James version of the Bible gave them a unique resonance, and it is worth analysing some of the ways in which its translators achieved this. Imbued with the language of Shakespeare, the translators of the 1611 Bible brilliantly utilized the bard's own rhetorical devices to maximize the impact of the precious words they were bringing anew before English men and women. One pattern of speech, in Shakespeare and the Bible, is to increase the length of any succession of phrases or syllables for greater impact. So Shakespeare in Julius Caesar begins a famous speech with the words, 'Friends, Romans, countrymen' (one syllable, two syllables, three syllables).

The same technique is subtly deployed in the King James Bible in, for instance, a summary by the prophet Micah of what God demands of us: 'to do justly, and to love mercy, and to walk humbly with thy God' (four syllables, five syllables and eight syllables).

Variations on this technique appear again and again in the prose and poetry of the King James Bible. In the story of how Pharaoh's army drowned in the Red Sea, the King James Bible describes the army as Pharoah's 'horses, his chariots, and his horsemen' (two syllables, four syllables and four syllables). But then the King James Bible goes one better than Shakespeare's *Julius Caesar*, by slowing down the metre three verses later, when the waters are said to come 'upon the Egyptians, upon their chariots, and upon their horsemen' (six, six and five syllables). So they drown, their gradual exhaustion matched by the slackening tension of these syllables.

Another rhetorical device frequently deployed to heighten the tension in a story is to slow up the action by means of repetition (this time a device derived from the Scriptural text itself). So, for example, when Job hears of the disasters which have befallen his property and his family, each of the four messengers repeats the pathetic words 'and I only am escaped alone to tell thee'. Similarly, when King David anxiously enquires whether his son Absalom has survived a battle, although the reader knows that the young man is dead, David is made to repeat his question 'Is the young man Absalom safe?', while the messengers prevaricate, not wishing to bring bad tidings to their master.

Often this is no mere rhetorical device. Take for example King Solomon's most brilliant display of wisdom, when he is asked to judge which of two women is mother of a disputed baby. The account depicts Solomon repeating to himself the gist of the problem: 'Then said the king, The one saith, This is my son that liveth, and thy son is the dead: and the other saith, Nay; but thy son is the dead, and my son is the living.' Reading the text, we can virtually hear Solomon finding time to ponder, working out his response.

Throughout the Christian centuries the greatest artists have responded to the Scriptures. Some biblical stories have had an instant appeal to them, particularly those which depict viciousness or lasciviousness. Among the vicious, the tale of the youth David killing the giant Goliath and the story of Salome's mother successfully begging for the severed head of John the Baptist have inspired such masters as Claude Vignon and Benozzo Gozzoli.

As for lust, King David's overwhelming desire for Bathsheba, another man's wife, inspired Peter Paul Rubens, as did the tale of Samson beguiled by Delilah, a theme which chimed with a concept often found in sixteenth-century Netherlandish art, that of women dominating men. Ruben's depiction of Samson betrayed by Delilah is (in my view) among the finest of the paintings reproduced in this book, richly erotic, with a triumphant woman's face gloating over the humiliation of her lover, while the whole scene is nonetheless controlled by the biblical source on which it is based. As for the story of David's seduction of Bathsheba, Rubens has enriched his portrayal of this episode by including a snarling dog, whose presence indicates that only evil can ensue from the king's sin.

Tenderer notes are struck by idyllic scenes of Adam and Eve in the garden of Eden, of Ruth gleaning corn in the fields of her future husband Boaz, and of Jesus forgiving a woman taken in adultery. The Bible also reflects human grief, and to this theme superb artists, whose work is reproduced here, also responded, especially when they set about portraying the sufferings and crucifixion of Jesus.

As the theologian Austin Farrer wrote, 'To kill is the most powerful of human acts; and existence is annihilated at a stroke. At the sight of death we catch our breath and fear.' Death and the conquest of death are perennial themes of the Bible. While many of the incidents and themes of this book can be appreciated in an entirely secular frame of mind, the certainty of death and the hope of resurrection add transcendent elements to the Scriptures, two elements most movingly portrayed in Jesus's agony in the garden of Gethsemane before his own death and in the meeting between Mary Magdalen and her risen Lord.

Whether tender or vicious, angry or loving, cunning or open and trusting, each story included in this book is set against a classic painting, some of them well-known, some rarely reproduced.

And in compiling this anthology I have deliberately not set out the scriptural passages and works of art in a chronological sequence ending with Jesus, in part so as not to promulgate Christian triumphalism – as if everything in earlier scriptures were inferior to what he taught and exemplified. Each passage and painting stands in its own right, though clearly enriched by the meditation of later centuries. Sometimes I have felt free to put a Christian gloss on an earlier Jewish text, as for example setting a picture of Jesus as a shepherd alongside Psalm 23 (since Jesus specifically compared himself to a shepherd); but in doing so in no way do I wish to suggest that the Jewish scriptures are meaningless unless interpreted through Jesus. Every excerpt in this anthology has its own authenticity.

Writing his sketch of the life of John Bunyan in 1878, James Anthony Froude observed that 'The Bible, thoroughly known, is a literature of itself', adding that it constitutes 'the rarest and richest in all departments of thought or imagination which exists'. My joy has been to set this greatest of translations against some of the most visionary works of art ever painted.

JAMES BENTLEY

Herbert Gustave Schmalz (b.1856),
*The Daughters of Judah in Babylon* (detail).

# GRIEF

Few books have so poignantly expressed human grief as the Bible. Unless grief is fully felt, the promise of comfort is no great thing. The hope of resurrection is of little worth unless the pain of death is unendurable.

Grief at the death of friends or children is a repeated Scriptural theme, inspiring to the peak of their powers poets such as King David (lamenting the loss of his son Absalom and his friend Jonathan). Grief brings Mary Magdalen in tears to Jesus's tomb.

In the Bible grief is also displayed by those who have fallen short in some way; a sinful woman weeping before the feet of Jesus; a king too weak to prevent the beheading of John the Baptist; St Peter afraid to admit his connection with Jesus.

And Jesus himself, according to the gospel of Mark, fell into despair on the cross, supposing that God had finally forsaken him.

# King David Laments the Death of Jonathan

The beauty of Israel is slain upon thy high places: how are the mighty fallen!

Tell it not in Gath, publish it not in the streets of Askelon, lest the daughters of the Philistines rejoice, lest the daughters of the uncircumcised triumph.

Ye mountains of Gilboa, let there be no dew, neither let there be rain, upon you, nor fields of offerings: for there the shield of the mighty is vilely cast away, the shield of Saul, as though he had not been anointed with oil.

From the blood of the slain, from the fat of the mighty, the bow of Jonathan turned not back, and the sword of Saul returned not empty.

Saul and Jonathan were lovely and pleasant in their lives, and in their death they were not divided: they were swifter than eagles, they were stronger than lions.

Ye daughters of Israel, weep over Saul, who clothed you in scarlet, with other delights, who put on ornaments of gold upon your apparel.

How are the mighty fallen in the midst of battle! O Jonathan, thou wast slain in thine high places.

I am distressed for thee, my brother Jonathan: very pleasant hast thou been to me: thy love to me was wonderful, passing the love of women.

How are the mighty fallen, and the weapons of war perished!

II Samuel chapter 1, verses 19 to 27.

PROPHAETA . DAVID .

FRA ANGELICO (*C.*1400–1455)
*KING DAVID PLAYING THE HARP.*

CAREL FABRITIUS (1622–1654),
*THE RAISING OF LAZARUS.*

# The Death of Lazarus

Now a certain man was sick, named Lazarus, of Bethany, the town of Mary and her sister Martha.

(It was that Mary which anointed the Lord with ointment, and wiped his feet with her hair, whose brother Lazarus was sick.)

Therefore his sisters sent unto him, saying, Lord, behold, he whom thou lovest is sick.

When Jesus heard that, he said, This sickness is not unto death, but for the glory of God, that the Son of God might be glorified thereby.

Now Jesus loved Martha, and her sister, and Lazarus.

When he had heard therefore that he was sick, he abode two days still in the same place where he was.

Then after that saith he to his disciples, Let us go into Judaea again. . .

Then when Mary was come where Jesus was, and saw him, she fell down at his feet, saying unto him, Lord, if thou hadst been here, my brother had not died.

When Jesus therefore saw her weeping, and the Jews also weeping which came with her, he groaned in the spirit and was troubled,

And said, Where have ye laid him? They said unto him, Lord, come and see.

Jesus wept.

Then said the Jews, Behold how he loved him!

And some of them said, Could not this man, which opened the eyes of the blind, have caused that even this man should not have died?

Jesus therefore again groaning in himself cometh to the grave. It was a cave, and a stone lay upon it.

Jesus said, Take ye away the stone. Martha, the sister of him that was dead, saith unto him, Lord, by this time he stinketh: for he hath been dead four days.

Jesus saith unto her, Said I not unto thee, that, if thou wouldest believe, thou shouldest see the glory of God?

Then they took away the stone from the place where the dead was laid. And Jesus lifted up his eyes, and said, Father, I thank thee that thou has heard me.

And I knew that thou hearest me always: but because of the people which stand by I said it, that they may believe that thou hast sent me.

And when he thus had spoken, he cried with a loud voice, Lazarus, come forth.

And he that was dead came forth, bound hand and foot with graveclothes: and his face was bound about with a napkin. Jesus saith unto them, Loose him, and let him go.

Absalom rode upon a mule, and the mule went under the thick boughs of a great oak, and his head caught hold of the oak, and he was taken up between the heaven and the earth; and the mule that was under him went away.

And a certain man saw it, and told Joab, and said, Behold, I saw Absalom hanged in an oak. . .

Then said Joab to Cushi, Go tell the king what thou hast seen. And Cushi bowed himself unto Joab, and ran.

Then said Ahimaaz the son of Zadok yet again to Joab, But howsoever, let me, I pray thee, also run after Cushi. And Joab said, Wherefore wilt thou run, my son, seeing that thou has no tidings ready?

But howsoever, said he, let me run. And he said unto him, Run, Then Ahimaaz ran by the way of the plain, and overran Cushi.

And David sat between the two gates: and the watchman went up to the roof over the gate unto the wall, and lifted up his eyes, and looked, and behold a man running alone.

And the watchman cried, and told the king. And the king said, If he be alone, there is tidings in his mouth. And he came apace, and drew near.

And the watchman saw another man running; and the watchman called unto the porter, and said, Behold another man running alone. And the king said, He also bringeth tidings.

And the watchman said, Me thinketh the running of the foremost is like the running of Ahimaaz the son of Zadok. And the king said, He is a good man, and cometh with good tidings.

And Ahimaaz called, and said unto the king, All is well. And he fell down to the earth upon his face before the king, and said, Blessed be the Lord thy God, which hath delivered up the men that lifted up their hand against my lord the king.

And the king said, Is the young man Absalom safe? And Ahimaaz answered, When Joab sent the king's servant, and me thy servant, I saw a great tumult, but I knew not what it was.

And the king said unto him, Turn aside, and stand here. And he turned aside, and stood still.

And, behold, Cushi came; and Cushi said, Tidings, my lord the king: for the Lord hath avenged thee this day of all them that rose up against thee.

And the king said unto Cushi, Is the young man Absalom safe? And Cushi

II Samuel, chapter 18, verses 9 to 10 and 21 to 23; and chapter 19, verses 2 to 3.

answered, The enemies of my lord the king, and all that rise against thee to do thee hurt, be as that young man is.

And the king was much moved, and went up to the chamber over the gate, and wept: and as he went, thus he said, O my son Absalom, my son, my son Absalom! would God I had died for thee, O Absalom, my son, my son.

. . . And the victory that day was turned into mourning unto all the people: for the people heard say that day how the king was grieved for his son.

And the people gat them by stealth that day into the city, as people being ashamed steal away when they flee in battle.

Georges de la Tour (1593–1652),
*Job and his Wife.*

# JOB

There was a day when his sons and his daughters were eating and drinking wine in their eldest brother's house:

And there came a messenger unto Job, and said, The oxen were plowing, and the asses feeding beside them:
And the Sabeans fell upon them, and took them away; yea, they have slain the servants with the edge of the sword; and I only am escaped alone to tell thee.

While he was yet speaking, there came also another, and said, The fire of God is fallen from heaven, and hath burned up the sheep, and the servants, and consumed them; and I only am escaped alone to tell thee.

While he was yet speaking, there came also another, and said, The Chaldeans made out three bands, and fell upon the camels, and have carried them away, yea, and slain the servants with the edge of the sword: and I only am escaped alone to tell thee.

While he was yet speaking, there came also another, and said, Thy sons and thy daughters were eating and drinking wine in their eldest brother's house:

And, behold, there came a great wind from the wilderness, and smote the four corners of the house, and it fell upon the young men, and they are dead; and I only am escaped alone to tell thee.

Then Job arose, and rent his mantle, and shaved his head, and fell down upon the ground, and worshipped,

And said, Naked came I out of my mother's womb, and naked shall I return thither: the Lord gave, and the Lord hath taken away; blessed be the name of the Lord.

# The Suffering Servant

He is despised and rejected of men; a man of sorrows, and acquainted with grief: and we hid as it were our faces from him; he was despised, and we esteemed him not.

Surely he hath borne our griefs, and carried our sorrows: yet we did esteem him stricken, smitten of God, and afflicted.

But he was wounded for our transgressions, he was bruised for our iniquities: the chastisement of our peace was upon him; and with his stripes we are healed.

All we like sheep have gone astray; we have turned every one to his own way; and the Lord hath laid on him the iniquity of us all.

He was oppressed, and he was afflicted, yet he opened not his mouth: he is brought as a lamb to the slaughter, and as a sheep before her shearers is dumb, so he openeth not his mouth.

He was taken from prison and from judgment: and who shall declare his generation? for he was cut off out of the land of the living: for the transgression of my people was he stricken.

And he made his grave with the wicked, and with the rich in his death; because he had done no violence, neither was any deceit in his mouth.

Yet it pleased the Lord to bruise him; he hath put him to grief.

HERBERT GUSTAVE SCHMALZ (B.1856),
*THE DAUGHTERS OF JUDAH IN BABYLON.*

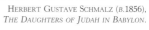

# The Jews Lament in Exile

By the rivers of Babylon, there we sat down, yea, we wept, when we remembered Zion.

We hanged our harps upon the willows in the midst thereof.

For there they that carried us away captive required of us a song; and they that wasted us required of us mirth, saying, Sing us one of the songs of Zion.

How shall we sing the Lord's song in a strange land?

If I forget thee, O Jerusalem, let my right hand forget her cunning.

If I do not remember thee, let my tongue cleave to the roof of my mouth; if I prefer not Jerusalem above my chief joy.

Remember, O Lord, the children of Edom in the day of Jerusalem; who said, Rase it, rase it, even to the foundation thereof.

O daughter of Babylon, who art to be destroyed; happy shall he be, that rewardeth thee as thou hast served us.

Happy shall he be, that taketh and dasheth thy little ones against the stones.

# The Slaughter of the Innocents

Now when Jesus was born in Bethlehem of Judaea in the days of Herod the king, behold, there came wise men from the east to Jerusalem,

Saying, Where is he that is born King of the Jews? for we have seen his star in the east, and are come to worship him.

When Herod the king had heard these things, he was troubled, and all Jerusalem with him.

And when he had gathered all the chief priests and scribes of the people together, he demanded of them where Christ should be born.

And they said unto him, In Bethlehem of Judaea: for thus it is written by the prophet,

And thou, Bethlehem, in the land of Juda, art not the least among the princes of Juda: for out of thee shall come a Governor, that shall rule my people Israel.

Then Herod, when he had privily called the wise men, inquired of them diligently what time the star appeared.

And he sent them to Bethlehem, and said, Go and search diligently for the young child; and when ye have found him, bring me word again, that I may come and worship him also . . .

And being warned of God in a dream that they should not return to Herod, they departed into their own country another way . . .

Then Herod, when he saw that he was mocked of the wise men, was exceeding wroth, and sent forth, and slew all the children that were in Bethlehem, and in all the coasts thereof, from two years old and under, according to the time which he had diligently inquired of the wise men.

Then was fulfilled that which was spoken by Jeremy the prophet, saying,

In Rama was there a voice heard, lamentation, and weeping, and great mourning, Rachel weeping for her children, and would not be comforted, because they are not.

Matthew chapter 2, verses 1 to 8, 12, and 16 to 18.

RATVS ERODES OCCIDIT OMNES PVEROS QVI ERAT INBETHELEHEM. MACEL. II. C

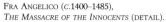

FRA ANGELICO (*c*.1400–1485),
*THE MASSACRE OF THE INNOCENTS* (DETAIL).

FOLLOWER OF DIERIC BOUTS (15TH CENTURY),
*CHRIST IN THE HOUSE OF SIMON THE PHARISEE.*

# A Sinful Woman Weeps Beside Jesus

And one of the Pharisees desired [Jesus] that he would eat with him. And he went into the Pharisee's house, and sat down to meat.

And, behold, a woman in the city, which was a sinner, when she knew that Jesus sat at meat in the Pharisee's house, brought an alabaster box of ointment.

And stood at his feet behind him weeping, and began to wash his feet with tears, and did wipe them with the hairs of her head, and kissed his feet, and anointed them with the ointment.

Now when the Pharisee which had bidden him saw it, he spake within himself, saying, This man, if he were a prophet, would have known who and what manner of woman this is that toucheth him: for she is a sinner.

And Jesus answering said unto him, Simon, I have somewhat to say unto thee. And he saith, Master, say on.

There was a certain creditor which had two debtors: the one owed five hundred pence, and the other fifty.

And when they had nothing to pay, he frankly forgave them both. Tell me therefore, which of them will love him most?

Simon answered and said, I suppose that he, to whom he forgave most. And he said unto him, Thou has rightly judged.

And he turned to the woman, and said unto Simon, Seest thou this woman? I entered into thine house, thou gavest me no water for my feet: but she hath washed my feet with tears, and wiped them with the hairs of her head.

Thou gavest me no kiss: but this woman since the time I came in hath not ceased to kiss my feet.

My head with oil thou didst not anoint: but this woman hath anointed my feet with ointment.

Wherefore I say unto thee, Her sins, which are many, are forgiven; for she loved much: but to whom little is forgiven, the same loveth little.

And he said unto her, Thy sins are forgiven.

And they that sat at meat with him began to say within themselves,

Who is this that forgiveth sins also? And he said to the woman, Thy faith hath saved thee; go in peace.

# The Beheading of John the Baptist

Herod himself had sent forth and laid hold upon John, and bound him in prison for Herodias' sake, his brother Philip's wife: for he had married her.

For John had said unto Herod, It is not lawful for thee to have thy brother's wife.

Therefore Herodias had a quarrel against him, and would have killed him; but she could not:

For Herod feared John, knowing that he was a just man and an holy, and observed him; and when he heard him, he did many things, and heard him gladly.

And when a convenient day was come, that Herod on his birthday made a supper to his lords, high captains, and chief estates of Galilee;

And when the daughter of the said Herodias came in, and danced, and pleased Herod and them that sat with him, the king said unto the damsel, Ask of me whatsoever thou wilt, and I will give it thee.

And he sware unto her, Whatsoever thou shalt ask of me, I will give thee, unto the half of my kingdom.

And she went forth, and said unto her mother, What shall I ask? And she said, The head of John the Baptist.

And she came in straightway with haste unto the king, and asked, saying, I will that thou give me by and by in a charger the head of John the Baptist.

And the king was exceeding sorry; yet for his oath's sake, and for their sakes which sat with him, he would not reject her.

And immediately the king sent an executioner, and commanded his head to be brought: and he went and beheaded him in the prison,

And brought his head in a charger, and gave it to the damsel: and the damsel gave it to her mother.

And when his disciples heard of it, they came and took up his corpse, and laid it in a tomb.

Mark chapter 6, verses 17 to 29.

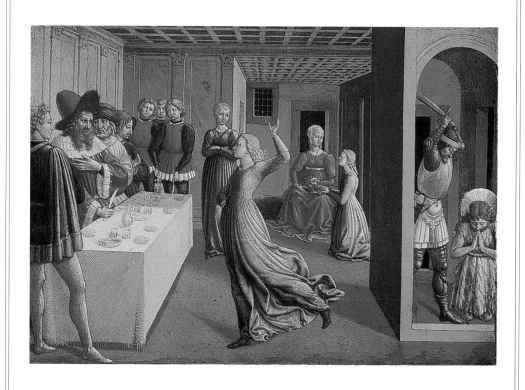

GEORGES DE LA TOUR (1593–1652),
*ST PETER'S DENIAL*.

# Peter Denies his Friendship with Jesus

Then they took [Jesus], and led him, and brought him into the high priest's house. And Peter followed afar off.

And when they had kindled a fire in the midst of the hall, and were set down together, Peter sat down among them.

But a certain maid beheld him as he sat by the fire, and earnestly looked upon him, and said, This man was also with him.

And he denied him, saying, Woman, I know him not.

And after a little while another saw him, and said, Thou art also of them. And Peter said, Man, I am not.

And about the space of one hour after another confidently affirmed, saying, Of a truth, this fellow also was with him: for he is a Galilaean.

And Peter said, Man, I know not what thou sayest. And immediately, while he yet spake, the cock crew.

And the Lord turned, and looked upon Peter. And Peter remembered the word of the Lord, how he had said unto him, Before the cock crow, thou shalt deny me thrice.

And Peter went out, and wept bitterly.

# The Garden of Gethsemane

Then cometh Jesus with them unto a place called Gethsemane, and saith unto the disciples, Sit ye here, while I go and pray yonder.

And he took with him Peter and the two sons of Zebedee, and began to be sorrowful and very heavy.

Then saith he unto them, My soul is exceedingly sorrowful, even unto death: tarry ye here, and watch with me.

And he went a little further, and fell on his face, and prayed, saying, O my father, if it be possible, let this cup pass from me: nevertheless not as I will, but as thou wilt.

And he cometh unto the disciples, and findeth them asleep, and saith unto Peter, What, could ye not watch with me one hour?

Watch and pray, that ye enter not into temptation: the spirit indeed is willing, but the flesh is weak.

He went away again the second time, and prayed, saying, O my Father, if this cup may not pass away from me, except I drink it, thy will be done.

And he came and found them asleep again: for their eyes were heavy.

And he left them, and went away again, and prayed the third time, saying the same words.

SANDRO BOTTICELLI (1444–1510),
*THE AGONY IN THE GARDEN.*

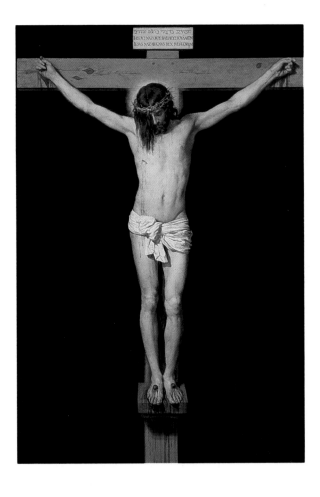

VELÁZQUEZ (1599–1660),
*CRUCIFIXION.*

They bring him unto the place Golgotha, which is, being interpreted, The place of a skull.

And they gave him to drink wine mingled with myrrh: but he received it not.

And when they had crucified him, they parted his garments, casting lots upon them, what every man should take.

And it was the third hour, and they crucified him.

And the superscription of his accusation was written over, THE KING OF THE JEWS.

And with him they crucify two thieves; the one on his right hand, and other on his left.

And the scripture was fulfilled, which saith, And he was numbered with the transgressors.

And they that passed by railed on him, wagging their heads, and saying, Ah, thou that destroyest the temple, and buildest it in three days,

Save thyself, and come down from the cross.

Likewise also the chief priests mocking said among themselves with the scribes, He saved others; himself he cannot save.

Let Christ the King of Israel descend now from the cross, that we may see and believe. And they that were crucified with him reviled him.

And when the sixth hour was come, there was darkness over the whole land until the ninth hour.

And at the ninth hour Jesus cried with a loud voice, saying, Eloi, Eloi, lama sabachthani? which is, being interpreted, My God, my God, why hast thou forsaken me?

And some of them that stood by, when they heard it, said, Behold, he calleth Elias.

And one ran and filled a spunge full of vinegar, and put it on a reed, and gave him to drink, saying, Let alone; let us see whether Elias will come to take him down.

And Jesus cried with a loud voice, and gave up the ghost.

Mary stood without at the sepulchre weeping: and as she wept, she stooped down, and looked into the sepulchre,

And seeth two angels in white sitting, the one at the head, and the other at the feet, where the body of Jesus had lain.

And they say unto her, Woman, why weepest thou? She saith unto them, Because they have taken away my Lord, and I know not where they have laid him.

And when she had thus said, she turned herself back, and saw Jesus standing, and knew not that it was Jesus.

Jesus saith unto her, Woman, why weepest thou? whom seekest thou? She, supposing him to be the gardener, saith unto him, Sir, if thou have borne him hence, tell me where thou hast laid him, and I will take him away.

Jesus saith unto her, Mary. She turned herself, and saith unto him, Rabboni; which is to say, Master.

Jesus saith unto her, Touch me not; for I am not yet ascended to my Father: but go to my brethren, and say unto them, I ascend unto my Father, and your Father; and to my God, and your God.

John chapter 20, verses 11 to 17.

RAPHAEL (1483–1520),
*THE HOLY FAMILY WITH A LAMB* (DETAIL).

# COMFORT

'Even the youths shall faint and be weary, and the young men shall utterly fall', declared the prophet Isaiah, adding, 'But they that wait upon the Lord shall renew their strength.'

Divine comfort is a theme that threads its way through the Bible. The prophet Elijah, longing for death, is sustained by heaven-sent ravens who bring him food. God himself, we are assured, shall behave to his children as a shepherd guards his flock. Even those who have committed great sins shall be forgiven. The unjustly persecuted shall have their reward in heaven. In heaven, we are promised, God shall wipe away all tears from our eyes.

Alongside this comes a moral demand. In response to God's loving kindness, human beings in their turn are required to comfort those in trouble. Even a tiny gesture (such as the kindness shown by those who, when pulling Jeremiah out of a dungeon, thought to place old rags under his painful armholes) is of value in the sight both of human beings and of God. Traditional enmities, between wild animals, for instance, shall disappear, and a little child shall control the beasts of the field (which is why artists so often portray the infant Jesus placidly riding on a lamb).

# Elijah is Sustained by God

Elijah the Tishbite, who was of the inhabitants of Gilead, said unto Ahab, As the Lord God of Israel liveth, before whom I stand, there shall not be dew nor rain these years, but according to my word.

And the word of the Lord came unto him, saying,

Get thee hence, and turn thee eastward, and hide thyself by the brook Cherith, that is before Jordan.

And it shall be, that thou shalt drink of the brook; and I have commanded the ravens to feed thee there. . .

And Ahab told Jezebel all that Elijah had done, and withal how he had slain all the prophets with the sword.

Then Jezebel sent a messenger unto Elijah, saying, So let the gods do to me, and more also, if I make not thy life as the life of one of them by tomorrow about this time.

And when he saw that, he arose, and went for his life, and came to Beersheba, which belongeth to Judah, and left his servant there.

But he himself went a day's journey into the wilderness, and came and sat down under a juniper tree: and he requested for himself that he might die; and said, It is enough; now, O Lord, take away my life;

for I am not better than my fathers.

And as he lay and slept under a juniper tree, behold, then an angel touched him, and said unto him, Arise and eat.

And he looked, and behold, there was a cake baken on the coals, and a cruse of water at his head. And he did eat and drink, and laid him down again.

And the angel of the Lord came again the second time, and touched him, and said, Arise and eat; because the journey is too great for thee.

And he arose, and did eat and drink, and went in the strength of that meat forty days and forty nights unto Horeb the mount of God.

And he came thither unto a cave, and lodged there; and, behold, the word of the Lord came to him, and he said unto him, What doest thou here, Elijah?

And he said, I have been very jealous for the Lord God of hosts: for the children of Israel have forsaken thy covenant, thrown down thine altars, and slain thy prophets with the sword; and I, even I only, am left; and they seek my life, to take it away.

And he said, Go forth, and stand up on the mount before the Lord. And, behold, the Lord passed by, and a great and strong

I Kings chapter 17, verses 1 to 3,
and chapter 19, verses 1 to 13.

wind rent the mountains, and brake in pieces the rocks before the Lord; but the Lord was not in the wind: and after the wind an earthquake; but the Lord was not in the earthquake:

And after the earthquake a fire; but the Lord was not in the fire: and after the fire a still small voice.

And it was so, when Elijah heard it, that he wrapped his face in his mantle, and went out.

PIETRO PERUGINO (*c*.1445–1523),
*THE PROPHET ISAIAH.*

# ISAIAH PREACHES COMFORT

Comfort ye, comfort ye my people, saith your God.

Speak ye comfortably to Jerusalem, and cry unto her, that her warfare is accomplished, that her iniquity is pardoned: for she hath received of the Lord's hand double for all her sins.

The voice of him that crieth in the wilderness, Prepare ye the way of the Lord, make straight in the desert a highway for our God.

Every valley shall be exalted, and every mountain and hill shall be made low: and the crooked shall be made straight, and the rough places plain:

And the glory of the Lord shall be revealed, and all flesh shall see it together: for the mouth of the Lord hath spoken it.

The voice said, Cry. And he said, What shall I cry? All flesh is grass, and all the goodliness thereof is as the flower of the field:

The grass withereth, the flower fadeth: because the spirit of the Lord bloweth upon it: surely the people is grass.

The grass withereth, the flower fadeth: but the word of our God shall stand for ever.

O Zion, that bringest good tidings, get thee up into the high mountain; O Jerusalem, that bringest good tidings, lift up thy voice with strength; lift it up, be not afraid; say unto the cities of Judah, Behold your God!

Behold, the Lord God will come with strong hand, and his arm shall rule for him: behold, his reward is with him, and his work before him.

He shall feed his flock like a shepherd: he shall gather the lambs with his arm, and carry them in his bosom, and shall gently lead those that are with young. . .

He giveth power to the faint; and to them that have no might he increaseth strength.

Even the youths shall faint and be weary, and the young men shall utterly fall:

But they that wait upon the Lord shall renew their strength; they shall mount up with wings as eagles; they shall run, and not be weary; and they shall walk and not faint.

# The Power of Evil Broken

And there was war in heaven: Michael and his angels fought against the dragon; and the dragon fought and his angels,

And prevailed not; neither was their place found any more in heaven.

And the great dragon was cast out, that old serpent, called the Devil, and Satan, which deceiveth the whole world: he was cast out into the earth, and his angels were cast out with him.

And I heard a loud voice saying in heaven, Now is come salvation, and strength, and the kingdom of our God, and the power of his Christ: for the accuser of our brethren is cast down, which accused them before our God day and night.

And they overcame him by the blood of the Lamb, and by the word of their testimony; and they loved not their lives unto the death.

Therefore rejoice, ye heavens, and ye that dwell in them. Woe to the inhabiters of the earth and of the sea! for the devil is come down unto you, having great wrath, because he knoweth that he hath but a short time.

BARTOLOMÉ BERMEJO (*FL.* 1474–1498),
*ST MICHAEL AND THE DRAGON* (DETAIL).

RAPHAEL (1483–1520),
*THE HOLY FAMILY WITH A LAMB.*

And there shall come forth a rod out of the stem of Jesse, and a Branch shall grow out of his roots:

And the spirit of the Lord shall rest upon him, the spirit of wisdom and understanding, the spirit of counsel and might, the spirit of knowledge and of the fear of the Lord;. . .

With righteousness shall he judge the poor, and reprove with equity for the meek of the earth: and he shall smite the earth with the rod of his mouth, and with the breath of his lips shall he slay the wicked.

And righteousness shall be the girdle of his loins, and faithfulness the girdle of his reins.

The wolf shall also dwell with the lamb, and the leopard shall lie down with the kid; and the calf and the young lion and the fatling together; and a little child shall lead them.

And the cow and the bear shall feed; their young ones shall lie down together; and the lion shall eat straw like the ox.

And the sucking child shall play on the hole of the asp, and the weaned child shall put his hand on the cockatrice' den.

They shall not hurt or destroy in all my holy mountain: for the earth shall be full of the knowledge of the Lord, as the waters cover the sea.

Isaiah chapter 11, verses 1 to 2 and 4 to 9.

# GOD AS A SHEPHERD

A PSALM OF DAVID

The Lord is my shepherd; I shall not want.

He maketh me to lie down in green pastures: he leadeth me beside the  still waters.

He restoreth my soul: he leadeth me in the paths of righteousness for his name's sake.

Yea, though I walk through the valley of the shadow of death, I will fear no evil: for thou art with me; thy rod and thy staff they comfort me.

Thou preparest a table before me in the presence of mine enemies; thou anointest my head with oil; my cup runneth over.

Surely goodness and mercy shall follow me all the days of my life: and I will dwell in the house of the Lord for ever.

FRANS FRANCKEN THE YOUNGER (1581–1642),
*CHRIST AND THE WOMAN TAKEN IN ADULTERY* (DETAIL).

# A Woman Caught Committing Adultery

Jesus went unto the Mount of Olives.

And early in the morning he came again into the temple, and all the people came unto him; and he sat down and taught them.

And the scribes and Pharisees brought unto him a woman taken in adultery; and when they had set her in the midst,

They say unto him, Master, this woman was taken in adultery, in the very act.

Now Moses in the law commanded us, that such should be stoned: but what sayest thou?

This they said, tempting him, that they might have to accuse him. But Jesus stooped down, and with his finger wrote on the ground, as though he heard them not.

So when they continued asking him, he lifted up himself, and said unto them, He that is without sin among you, let him first cast a stone at her.

And again he stooped down, and wrote on the ground.

And they which heard it, being convicted by their own conscience, went out one by one, beginning at the eldest, even unto the last: and Jesus was left alone, and the woman standing in the midst.

When Jesus had lifted up himself, and saw none but the woman, he said unto her, Woman, where are those thine accusers? hath no man condemned thee?

She said, No man, Lord. And Jesus said unto her, Neither do I condemn thee: go, and sin no more.

# The Annunciation to the Shepherds

And there were in the same country shepherds abiding in the field, keeping watch over their flock by night.

And, lo, the angel of the Lord came upon them, and the glory of the Lord shone round about them: and they were sore afraid.

And the angel said unto them, Fear not: for, behold, I bring you good tidings of great joy, which shall be to all people.

For unto you is born this day in the city of David a Saviour, which is Christ the Lord.

And this shall be a sign unto you; Ye shall find the babe wrapped in swaddling clothes, lying in a manger.

And suddenly there was with the angel a multitude of the heavenly host praising God, and saying,

Glory to God in the highest, and on earth peace, good will toward men.

And it came to pass, as the angels were gone away from them into heaven, the shepherds said one to another, Let us now go even unto Bethlehem, and see this thing which is come to pass, which the Lord hath made known unto us.

And they came with haste, and found Mary, and Joseph, and the babe, lying in a manger.

And when they had seen it, they made known abroad the saying which was told them concerning this child.

And all they that heard it wondered at those things which were told them by the shepherds.

But Mary kept all these things, and pondered them in her heart.

And the shepherds returned, glorifying and praising God for all the things that they had heard and seen, as it was told unto them.

Luke chapter 2, verses 8 to 20.

ANNUNCIATION TO THE SHEPHERDS, FROM
*A FRENCH BOOK OF HOURS, C.*1470.
BRITISH LIBRARY, LONDON

57

LUCA GIORDANO (1634–1705),
*THE GOOD SAMARITAN.*

# The Good Samaritan

But he . . . said unto Jesus, And who is my neighbour?

And Jesus answering said, A certain man went down from Jerusalem to Jericho, and fell among thieves, which stripped him of his raiment, and wounded him, and departed, leaving him half dead.

And by chance there came down a certain priest that way: and when he saw him, he passed by on the other side.

And likewise a Levite, when he was at the place, came and looked on him, and passed by on the other side.

But a certain Samaritan, as he journeyed, came where he was: and when he saw him, he had compassion on him,'

And went to him, and bound up his wounds, pouring in oil and wine, and set him on his own beast, and brought him to an inn, and took care of him.

And on the morrow when he departed, he took out two pence, and gave them to the host, and said unto him, Take care of him; whatsoever thou spendest more, when I come again, I will repay thee.

Which now of these three, thinkest thou, was neighbour unto him that fell among the thieves?

And he said, He that shewed mercy on him. Then said Jesus unto him, Go, and do thou likewise.

Luke chapter 10, verses 29 to 37.

# THE BEATITUDES

And seeing the multitudes, Jesus went up into a mountain: and when he was set, his disciples came unto him:

And he opened his mouth, and taught them, saying,

Blessed are the poor in spirit: for theirs is the kingdom of heaven.

Blessed are they that mourn: for they shall be comforted.

Blessed are the meek: for they shall inherit the earth.

Blessed are they which do hunger and thirst after righteousness: for they shall be filled.

Blessed are the merciful: for they shall obtain mercy.

Blessed are the pure in heart: for they shall see God.

Blessed are the peacemakers: for they shall be called the children of God.

Blessed are they which are persecuted for righteousness' sake: for theirs is the kingdom of heaven.

Blessed are ye, when men shall revile you, and persecute you, and shall say all manner of evil against you falsely, for my sake.

Rejoice, and be exceeding glad: for great is your reward in heaven: for so persecuted they the prophets which were before you.

Joos Momper the Younger (1564–1635),
*The Sermon on the Mount* (detail).

61

GIOVANNI DOMENICO TIEPOLO (1727–1804),
*CHRIST ON THE CROSS.*

## SUCCOUR IN SUFFERING

There were also two other malefactors, led with [Jesus] to be put to death.

And when they were come to the place, which is called Calvary, there they crucified him, and the malefactors, one on the right hand, and the other on the left.

Then said Jesus, Father, forgive them; for they know not what they do. And they parted his raiment, and cast lots.

And the people stood beholding. And the rulers also with them derided him, saying, He saved others; let him save himself, if he be Christ, the chosen of God.

And the soldiers also mocked him, coming to him, and offering him vinegar,

And saying, If thou be the king of the Jews, save thyself.

And a superscription also was written over him in letters of Greek, and Latin, and Hebrew, THIS IS THE KING OF THE JEWS.

And one of the malefactors which were hanged railed on him, saying, If thou be Christ, save thyself and us.

But the other answering rebuked him, saying, Dost not thou fear God, seeing thou art in the same condemnation?

And we indeed justly; for we receive the due reward of our deeds: but this man hath done nothing amiss.

And he said unto Jesus, Lord, remember me when thou comest into thy kingdom.

And Jesus said unto him, Verily I say unto thee, Today shalt thou be with me in paradise.

# JEREMIAH, PUNISHED AND COMFORTED

Then the word of the Lord came to Jeremiah. . . saying,

And thou shalt say to Jehoiakim, king of Judah, Thus saith the Lord. . ., The king of Babylon shall certainly come and destroy this land. . .

Therefore the princes said unto the king, We beseech thee, let this man be put to death: for thus he weakeneth the hands of the men of war that remain in this city, and the hands of all the people, in speaking such words unto them: for this man seeketh not the welfare of this people, but the hurt.

Then. . . the king said, Behold, he is in your hand: for the king is not he that can do any thing against you.

Then took they Jeremiah, and cast him into the dungeon of Malchiah the son of Hammelech, that was in the court of the prison: and they let down Jeremiah with cords. And in the dungeon there was no water, but mire: so Jeremiah sunk in the mire.

Now when Ebedmelech the Ethiopian, one of the eunuchs which was in the king's house, heard that they had put Jeremiah in the dungeon; the king then sitting in the gate of Benjamin;

Ebedmelech went forth out of the king's house, and spake to the king, saying,

My lord the king, these men have done evil in all that they have done to Jeremiah the prophet, whom they have cast into the dungeon; and he is like to die for hunger in the place where he is: for there is no more bread in the city.

Then the king commanded Ebedmelech the Ethiopian, saying, Take from hence thirty men with thee, and take up Jeremiah the prophet out of the dungeon, before he die.

So Ebedmelech took the men with him, and went into the house of the king under the treasury, and took thence old cast clouts and old rotten rags, and let them down by cords into the dungeon to Jeremiah.

And Ebedmelech the Ethiopian said unto Jeremiah, Put now these old cast clouts and rotten rags under thine armholes under the cords. And Jeremiah did so.

So they drew up Jeremiah with cords, and took him up out of the dungeon.

Jeremiah chapter 36, verses 27 and 29, and chapter 38, verses 4 to 13.

MICHELANGELO (1475–1564),
*JEREMIAH,*
DETAIL FROM THE SISTINE CHAPEL CEILING.

65

WILLIAM BLAKE (1757–1827),
*JACOB'S LADDER.*

# Jacob's Dream

Jacob went out from Beersheba, and went toward Haran.

And he lighted upon a certain place, and tarried there all night, because the sun was set; and he took of the stones of that place, and put them for his pillows, and lay down in that place to sleep.

And he dreamed, and behold a ladder set up on the earth, and the top of it reached to heaven: and behold, the angels of God ascending and descending on it.

And, behold, the Lord stood above it, and said, I am the Lord God of Abraham thy father, and the God of Isaac: the land whereon thou liest, to thee will I give it, and to thy seed;

And thy seed shall be as the dust of the earth, and thou shalt spread abroad to the west, and to the east, and to the north, and to the south: and in thee shall all the families of the earth be blessed.

And, behold, I am with thee, and will keep thee in all places whither thou goest, and will bring thee again into this land; for I will not leave thee, until I have done that which I have spoken to thee of.

And Jacob awaked out of his sleep, and he said, Surely the Lord is in this place; and I knew it not.

# THE HEAVENLY JERUSALEM

After this I beheld, and, lo, a great multitude, which no man could number, of all nations, and kindreds, and people, and tongues, stood before the throne, and before the Lamb, clothed with white robes, and palms in their hands;

And cried with a loud voice, saying, Salvation to our God which sitteth upon the throne, and unto the Lamb.

And all the angels stood round about the throne, and about the elders and the four beasts, and fell before the throne on their faces, and worshipped God.

Saying, Amen: Blessing, and glory, and wisdom, and thanksgiving, and honour, and power, and might, be unto our God for ever and ever. Amen.

And one of the elders answered, saying unto me, What are these which are arrayed in white robes? and whence came they?

And I said unto him, Sir, thou knowest. And he said to me, These are they which came out of great tribulation, and have washed their robes, and made them white in the blood of the Lamb.

Therefore are they before the throne of God, and serve him day and night in his temple: and he that sitteth on the throne shall dwell among them.

They shall hunger no more, neither thirst any more; neither shall the sun light on them, nor any heat.

For the Lamb which is in the midst of the throne shall feed them, and shall lead them unto living fountains of waters: and God shall wipe away all tears from their eyes.

Jaime Ferrer (15th century),
The Last Judgment, Altarpiece from the church of
Sant Salvador d'Albaterrec, Lleida.

69

J. B. PRATT, 1892,
MEZZOTINT AFTER BRITON RIVIÈRE,
*DANIEL IN THE LIONS' DEN* (DETAIL).

# FAITH

We can read the Bible for its secular stories and earthly wisdom; but intertwined with these is the supernatural, the notion of an ineffable God, the presumption of eternal life. Yet since the books of the Bible were written by earthly men and women, the possibility that there is more than this material life remains only a promise, not a reality. In consequence, throughout its pages the Bible shows men and women doubting as well as believing.

Some are vouchsafed a vision of God. Remarkably, in the case of Isaiah in the Old Testament and the Virgin Mary in the New Testament, both feel first of all unworthy of such a vision, and secondly humbly accept whatever demands God should make of them.

Often the Bible presents faith as something irrational: Abraham willingly agrees to slaughter his son at God's command (though the command is later rescinded); three kings follow a star and fall down to worship an apparently insignificant child; St Paul, initially seeking to slaughter Christians, becomes one himself.

At other times faith is seen as trust in a God who will confound one's enemies, whatever the odds. Thus the young David kills Goliath and Daniel survives incarceration in a lions' den. Most irrational of all, yet most stubbornly clung to, is belief in a future life when dry bones will live; and Job claims that though worms destroy his body yet in his flesh he will see God.

## FAITH AS A GIFT

One of the multitude answered and said, Master, I have brought unto thee my son, which hath a dumb spirit;

And wheresoever he taketh him, he teareth him: and he foameth, and gnasheth with his teeth, and pineth away: and I spake to thy disciples that they should cast him out; and they could not.

He answereth him, and saith, O faithless generation, how long shall I be with you? how long shall I suffer you? bring him unto me.

And they brought him unto him: and when he saw him, straightway the spirit tare him; and he fell on the ground, and wallowed foaming.

And he asked his father, How long is it ago since this came unto him? And he said, Of a child.

And ofttimes it hath cast him into the fire, and into the waters, to destroy him: but if thou canst do any thing, have compassion on us, and help us.

Jesus said unto him, If thou canst believe, all things are possible to him that believeth.

And straightway the father of the child cried out, and said with tears, Lord, I believe; help thou mine unbelief.

When Jesus saw that the people came running together, he rebuked the foul spirit, saying unto him, Thou dumb and deaf spirit, I charge thee, come out of him, and enter no more into him.

And the spirit cried, and rent him sore, and came out of him: and he was as one dead; inasmuch that many said, He is dead.

But Jesus took him by the hand, and lifted him up; and he arose.

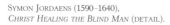
Symon Jordaens (1590–1640),
*Christ Healing the Blind Man* (detail).

GEORG PENCZ (1500–1550),
*DOUBTING THOMAS.*

# DOUBTING THOMAS

Thomas, one of the twelve, called Didymus, was not with them when Jesus came.

The other disciples therefore said unto him, We have seen the Lord. But he said unto them, Except I shall see in his hands the print of the nails, and put my finger into the print of the nails, and thrust my hand into his side, I will not believe.

And after eight days again his disciples were within, and Thomas with them: then came Jesus, the doors being shut, and stood in the midst, and said, Peace be unto you.

Then saith he to Thomas, Reach hither thy finger, and behold my hands; and reach hither thy hand, and thrust it into my side: and be not faithless, but believing.

And Thomas answered and said unto him, My Lord and my God.

Jesus saith unto him, Thomas, because thou hast seen me, thou hast believed: blessed are they that have not seen, and yet have believed.

# Isaiah's Vision in the Temple

In the year that King Uzziah died I saw also the Lord sitting upon a throne, high and lifted up, and his train filled the temple.

Above it stood the seraphims: each one had six wings; with twain he covered his face, and with twain he covered his feet, and with twain he did fly.

And one cried unto another, and said, Holy, holy, holy, is the Lord of hosts: the whole earth is full of his glory.

And the posts of the door moved at the voice of him that cried, and the house was filled with smoke.

Then said I, Woe is me, for I am undone, because I am a man of unclean lips, and I dwell in the midst of a people of unclean lips: for mine eyes have seen the king, the Lord of hosts.

Then flew one of the seraphims unto me, having a live coal in his hand, which he had taken with the tongs from off the altar:

And he laid it upon my mouth, and said, Lo, this hath touched thy lips; and thine iniquity is taken away, and thy sin purged.

Also I heard the voice of the Lord, saying, Whom shall I send, and who will go for us? Then said I, Here am I; send me.

Isaiah chapter 6, verses 1 to 8.

MATHIS GRÜNEWALD (C.1480–1528),
*THE PROPHET ISAIAH*,
FROM THE ISENHEIM ALTARPIECE.

The Master of the Annunciation (15th century),
*The Annunciation*, from the church of
Ste Marie Madeleine, Aix-en-Provence

# The Annunciation

And in the sixth month the angel Gabriel was sent from God unto a city of Galilee, named Nazareth,

To a virgin espoused to a man whose name was Joseph, of the house of David; and the virgin's name was Mary.

And the angel came in unto her, and said, Hail, thou that art highly favoured, the Lord is with thee: blessed art thou among women.

And when she saw him, she was troubled at his saying, and cast in her mind what manner of salutation this should be.

And the angel said unto her, Fear not, Mary: for thou hast found favour with God.

And, behold, thou shalt conceive in thy womb, and bring forth a son, and shalt call his name Jesus.

He shall be great, and shall be called the Son of the Highest: and the Lord God shall give unto him the throne of his father David:

And he shall reign over the house of Jacob for ever; and of his kingdom there shall be no end.

Then said Mary unto the angel, How shall this be, seeing I know not a man?

And the angel answered and said unto her, The Holy Ghost shall come upon thee, and the power of the Highest shall overshadow thee: therefore also that holy thing which shall be born of thee shall be called the Son of God . . .

And Mary said, Behold the handmaid of the Lord; be it unto me according to thy word.

Luke chapter 1, verses 26 to 35 and 38.

# A RAM CAUGHT IN A THICKET

And it came to pass after these things, that God did tempt Abraham, and said unto him, Abraham: and he said, Behold, here I am.

And he said, Take now thy son, thine only son Isaac, whom thou lovest, and get thee into the land of Moriah; and offer him there for a burnt offering upon one of the mountains which I will tell thee of . . .

And Isaac spoke unto Abraham his father, and said, My father: and he said, Here am I, my son. And he said, Behold the fire and the wood: but where is the lamb for a burnt offering?

And Abraham said, My son, God will provide himself a lamb for a burnt offering: so they went both of them together.

And they came to the place which God had told him of; and Abraham built an altar there, and laid the wood in order, and bound Isaac his son, and laid him on the altar upon the wood.

And Abraham stretched forth his hand, and took the knife to slay his son.

And the angel of the Lord called unto him out of heaven, and said, Abraham, Abraham: and he said, Here am I.

And he said, Lay not thine hand upon the lad, neither do thou any thing unto him: for now I know that thou fearest God, seeing that thou hast not withheld thy son, thine only son from me.

And Abraham lifted up his eyes, and looked, and behold behind him a ram caught in a thicket by his horns: and Abraham went and took the ram, and offered him up for a burnt offering in the stead of his son.

Genesis chapter 22, verse 1 to 2 and 7 to 13.

*ADORATION OF THE KINGS.*
OSTERREICHE NATIONALBIBLIOTHEK, VIENNA

# The Magi

Now when Jesus was born in Bethlehem of Judaea in the days of Herod the king, behold, there came wise men from the east to Jerusalem,

Saying, Where is he that is born King of the Jews? for we have seen his star in the east and are come to worship him . . .

And, lo, the star, which they saw in the east, went before them, till it came and stood over where the young child was.

When they saw the star, they rejoiced with exceeding great joy.

And when they were come into the house, they saw the young child with Mary his mother, and fell down, and worshipped him: and when they had opened their treasures, they presented unto him gifts; gold, and frankincense, and myrrh.

Joshua had commanded the people, saying, Ye shall not shout, nor make any noise with your voice, neither shall any word proceed out of your mouth, until the day I bid you shout; then shall ye shout.

So the ark of the Lord compassed the city, going about it once: and they came into the camp, and lodged in the camp.

And Joshua rose early in the morning, and the priests took up the ark of the Lord.

And seven priests bearing seven trumpets of rams' horns before the ark of the Lord went on continually, and blew with the trumpets: and the armed men went before them; but the rereward came after the ark of the Lord, the priests going on, and blowing with the trumpets.

And the second day they compassed the city once, and returned into the camp: so they did six days.

And it came to pass on the seventh day, that they rose early about the dawning of the day, and compassed the city after the same manner seven times: only on that day they compassed the city seven times.

And it came to pass at the seventh time, when the priests blew with the trumpets, Joshua said unto the people, Shout; for the Lord hath given you the city . . .

So the people shouted when the priests blew with the trumpets: and it came to pass, when the people heard the sound of the trumpet, and the people shouted with a great shout, that the wall fell down flat, so that the people went up into the city, every man straight before him, and they took the city.

And they utterly destroyed all that was in the city, both man and woman, young and old, and ox, and sheep, and ass, with the edge of the sword.

But Joshua had said unto the two men that had spied out the country, Go into the harlot's house, and bring out thence the woman, and all that she hath, as ye sware unto her . . .

And Joshua saved Rahab the harlot alive, and her father's household, and all that she had; and she dwelleth in Israel even unto this day; because she hid the messengers, which Joshua sent to spy out Jericho.

Joshua chapter 6, verses 10 to 16, 20 to 22, and 25.

JEAN FOUQUET (c.1420–80),
THE FALL OF JERICHO.

J. B. Pratt, 1892,
mezzotint after Briton Rivière,
*Daniel in the Lions' Den.*

# DANIEL IN THE LIONS' DEN

Then the king commanded, and they brought Daniel, and cast him into the den of lions. Now the king spake and said unto Daniel, Thy God whom thou servest continually, he will deliver thee.

And a stone was brought, and laid upon the mouth of the den; and the king sealed it with his own signet, and with the signet of his lords; that the purpose might not be changed concerning Daniel.

Then the king went to his palace, and passed the night fasting; neither were instruments of musick brought before him: and his sleep went from him.

Then the king arose very early in the morning, and went in haste unto the den of lions.

And when he came to the den, he cried with a lamentable voice unto Daniel: and the king spake and said to Daniel, O Daniel, servant of the living God, is thy God, whom thou servest continually, able to deliver thee from the lions?

Then said Daniel unto the king, O king, live for ever.

My God hath sent his angel, and hath shut the lions' mouths, that they have not hurt me: forasmuch as before him innocency was found in me; and also before thee, O king, have I done no hurt.

Then was the king exceeding glad for him, and commanded that they should take Daniel up out of the den. So Daniel was taken up out of the den, and no manner of hurt was found upon him, because he believed in his God.

And the king commanded, and they brought those men which had accused Daniel, and they cast them into the den of lions, them, their children, and their wives; and the lions had the mastery of them, and brake all their bones in pieces or ever they came at the bottom of the den.

Daniel chapter 6, verses 16 to 24.

# The Valley of Dry Bones

The hand of the Lord was upon me, and carried me out in the spirit of the Lord, and set me down in the midst of the valley which was full of bones,

And caused me to pass by them round about: and behold, there were very many in the open valley; and, lo, they were very dry.

And he said unto me, Son of man, can these bones live? And I answered, O Lord God, thou knowest.

Again he said unto me, Prophesy upon these bones, and say unto them, O ye dry bones, hear the word of the Lord.

Thus saith the Lord God unto these bones; Behold, I will cause breath to enter into you, and ye shall live:

And I will lay sinews upon you, and will bring up flesh upon you, and cover you with skin, and put breath in you, and ye shall live; and ye shall know that I am the Lord.

So I prophesied as I was commanded: and as I prophesied, there was a noise, and behold a shaking, and the bones came together, bone to his bone.

And when I beheld, lo, the sinews and the flesh came up upon them, and the skin covered them above: but there was no breath in them.

Then said he unto me, Prophesy unto the wind, prophesy, son of man, and say to the wind, Thus saith the Lord God; Come from the four winds, O breath, and breathe upon these slain, that they may live.

So I prophesied as he commanded me, and the breath came into them, and they lived, and stood up upon their feet, an exceeding great army.

Then he said unto me, Son of man, these bones are the whole house of Israel: behold, they say, Our bones are dried, and our hope is lost: we are cut off for our parts.

Therefore prophesy and say unto them, Thus saith the Lord God; Behold, O my people, I will open your graves, and cause you to come up out of your graves, and bring you into the land of Israel.

Ezekiel chapter 37, verses 1 to 12.

Francisco Collantes (1599–1656),
*The Vision of Ezekiel.*

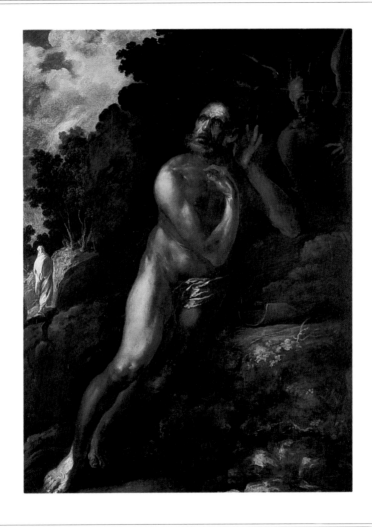

FRANCISCO HERRERA THE ELDER (1576–1656),
*JOB TEMPTED BY THE DEVIL.*

# JOB'S FAITH

Have pity upon me, have pity upon me, O ye my friends; for the hand of God hath touched me.

Why do ye persecute me as God, and are not satisfied with my flesh?

Oh that my words were now written! oh that they were printed in a book!

That they were graven with an iron pen and lead in the rock for ever!

For I know that my redeemer liveth, and that he shall stand at the latter day upon the earth:

And though after my skin worms destroy this body, yet in my flesh shall I see God:

Whom I shall see for myself, and mine eyes shall behold, and not another.

Job chapter 19, verses 25 to 27.

# MOSES DIVIDES THE WATERS

And when Pharaoh drew nigh, the children of Israel lifted up their eyes, and, behold, the Egyptians marched after them; and they were sore afraid: and the children of Israel cried out unto the Lord.

And they said unto Moses, Because there were no graves in Egypt, hast thou taken us away to die in the wilderness? . . .

And the Lord said unto Moses, Wherefore criest thou unto me? speak unto the children of Israel, that they go forward:

But lift thou up thy rod, and stretch out thine hand over the sea, and divide it: and the children of Israel shall go on dry ground through the midst of the sea . . .

And Moses stretched out his hand over the sea; and the Lord caused the sea to go back by a strong east wind all that night, and made the sea dry land, and the waters were divided.

And the children of Israel went into the midst of the sea upon the dry ground: and the waters were a wall unto them on their right hand, and on their left.

And the Egyptians pursued, and went in after them to the midst of the sea, even all Pharaoh's horses, his chariots, and his horsemen . . .

And Moses stretched forth his hand over the sea, and the sea returned to his strength when the morning appeared; and the Egyptians fled against it; and the Lord overthrew the Egyptians in the midst of the sea.

And the waters returned, and covered the chariots, and the horsemen, and all the hosts of Pharaoh that came into the sea after them; there remained not so much as one of them.

But the children of Israel walked upon dry land in the midst of the sea; and the waters were a wall unto them on their right hand, and on their left.

Thus the Lord saved Israel that day out of the hand of the Egyptians; and Israel saw the Egyptians dead upon the sea shore.

Exodus chapter 14, verses 10 to 11, 15 to 16, 21 to 23 and 27 to 30.

JACOB WILLEMSZ DE WET (C.1610–1672),
*THE PASSAGE OF THE RED SEA.*

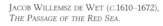

Claude Vignon (1593–1670),
*David with the Head of Goliath.*

# DAVID AND GOLIATH

[David] took his staff in his hand, and chose him five smooth stones out of the brook, and put them in a shepherd's bag which he had, even in a scrip; and his sling was in his hand: and he drew near to the Philistine.

And the Philistine came on and drew near unto David. And the man that bare the shield went before him.

And when the Philistine looked about, and saw David, he disdained him: for he was but a youth, and ruddy, and of a fair countenance.

And the Philistine said unto David, Am I a dog, that thou comest to me with staves? And the Philistine cursed David by his gods.

And the Philistine said to David, Come to me, and I will give thy flesh unto the fowls of the air, and to the beasts of the field.

Then said David to the Philistine, Thou comest to me with a sword, and with a spear, and with a shield: but I come to thee in the name of the Lord of hosts, the God of the armies of Israel, whom thou has defied .

. And it came to pass, when the Philistine arose, and came and drew nigh to meet David, that David hastened, and ran toward the army to meet the Philistine.

And David put his hand in his bag, and took thence a stone, and slang it, and smote the Philistine in his forehead, that the stone sunk into his forehead; and he fell upon his face to the earth.

So David prevailed over the Philistine with a sling and with a stone, and smote the Philistine, and slew him; but there was no sword in the hand of David.

Therefore David ran, and stood upon the Philistine, and took out his sword, and drew it out of the sheath thereof, and slew him, and cut off his head therewith. And when the Philistines saw their champion was dead, they fled.

I Samuel chapter 17, verses 40 to 45 and 48 to 51.

And Saul, yet breathing out threatenings and slaughter against the disciples of the Lord, went unto the high priest,

And desired of him letters to Damascus to the synagogues, that if he found any of this way, whether they were men or women, he might bring them bound unto Jerusalem.

And as he journeyed, he came near Damascus: and suddenly there shined round about him a light from heaven:

And he fell to the earth, and heard a voice saying unto him, Saul, Saul, why persecutest thou me?

And he said, Who art thou, Lord? And the Lord said, I am Jesus whom thou persecutest: it is hard for thee to kick against the pricks.

And he trembling and astonished said, Lord, what wilt thou have me to do? And the Lord said unto him, Arise, and go into the city, and it shall be told thee what thou must do.

And the men which journeyed with him stood speechless, hearing a voice, but seeing no man.

And Saul arose from the earth; and when his eyes were opened, he saw no man: but they led him by the hand, and brought him into Damascus.

Acts chapter 9, verses 1 to 8.

Pieter Brueghel the Elder (c.1515–1569),
*The Conversion of St Paul.*

JEAN FOUQUET (C.1420–1480),
THE CREATION: GOD PRESENTING EVE TO ADAM (DETAIL).

# LOVE

St Paul preached utterly disinterested love; charity, as it is translated in the King James Bible. His master Jesus taught his followers to care for the most insignificant person as if they were caring for him.

But these sublime precepts far from exhaust the biblical testimony to love, which is here represented in its infinite varieties.

The Bible begins with a paean to the love between men and women. In the story of Samson and Delilah it encapsulates betrayal; in the tale of Ruth and Boaz, tenderness; in its description of Jesus's family, filial obedience; in the saga of Joseph and Potiphar's wife, the savagery of a woman spurned; and in the narrative of David's seduction of Bathsheba, lust. The parable of the Prodigal Son speaks of a father's yearning for his errant child. The judgment of Solomon reveals a woman ready to lose her infant rather than see him killed. A woman named Mary is revealed to be besotted by Jesus and is not condemned for this. Finally, Jesus demands a new kind of love from St Peter, a loyalty more than he has ever before displayed.

# CHARITY

Though I speak with the tongues of men and of angels, and have not charity, I am become as sounding brass or a tinkling cymbal.

And though I have the gift of prophecy, and understand all mysteries, and all knowledge: and though I have all faith, so that I could remove mountains, and have not charity, I am nothing.

And though I bestow all my goods to feed the poor, and though I give my body to be burned, and have not charity, it profiteth me nothing.

Charity suffereth long, and is kind; charity envieth not; charity vaunteth not itself, is not puffed up.

Doth not behave itself unseemly, seeketh not her own, is not easily provoked, thinketh no evil;

Rejoiceth not in iniquity, but rejoiceth in the truth;

Beareth all things, believeth all things, hopeth all things, endureth all things.

Charity never faileth: but whether there be prophecies, they shall fail; whether there be tongues, they shall cease; whether there be knowledge, it shall vanish away.

For we know in part, and we prophesy in part.

But when that which is perfect is come, then that which is in part shall be done away.

When I was a child, I spake as a child, I understood as a child, I thought as a child: but when I became a man, I put away childish things.

For now we see through a glass, darkly; but then face to face: now I know in part; but then shall I know even as also I am known.

And now abideth faith, hope, charity, these three; but the greatest of these is charity.

I Corinthians chapter 13.

LUCAS VAN LEYDEN (*C.*1494–1533),
*THE LAST JUDGMENT*, ALTARPIECE.

# The Sheep and the Goats

When the Son of man shall come in his glory, and all the holy angels with him, then shall he sit upon the throne of his glory:

And before him shall be gathered all nations: and he shall separate them one from another, as a shepherd divideth his sheep from the goats:

And he shall set the sheep on his right hand, but the goats on the left.

Then shall the king say unto them on his right hand, Come, ye blessed of my Father, inherit the kingdom prepared for you from the foundation of the world:

For I was an hungred, and ye gave me meat: I was thirsty, and ye gave me drink: I was a stranger, and ye took me in:

Naked, and ye clothed me: I was sick, and ye visited me: I was in prison, and ye came unto me.

Then shall the righteous answer him, saying, Lord, when saw we thee an hungred, and fed thee? or thirsty, and gave thee drink?

When saw we thee a stranger, and took thee in? or naked, and clothed thee?

Or when saw we thee sick, or in prison, and came unto thee?

And the King shall answer and say unto them, Verily I say unto you, Inasmuch as ye have done it unto one of the least of these my brethren, ye have done it unto me.

Matthew chapter 25, verses 31 to 40.

# HUMAN LOVE

And the Lord God said, It is not good that the man should be alone; I will make him an help meet for him.

And out of the ground the Lord God formed every beast of the field, and every fowl of the air; and brought them unto Adam to see what he would call them: and whatsoever Adam called every living creature, that was the name thereof.

And Adam gave names to all cattle, and to the fowl of the air, and to every beast of the field; but for Adam there was not found an help meet for him.

And the Lord God caused a deep sleep to fall upon Adam, and he slept: and he took one of his ribs, and closed up the flesh instead thereof;

And the rib, which the Lord God had taken from man, made he a woman, and brought her unto the man.

And Adam said, This is now bone of my bones, and flesh of my flesh: she shall be called Woman, because she was taken out of Man.

Therefore shall a man leave his father and his mother, and shall cleave unto his wife: and they shall be one flesh.

And they were both naked, the man and his wife, and were not ashamed.

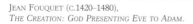

# SAMSON AND DELILAH

And it came to pass afterwards that [Samson] loved a woman in the valley of Sorek, whose name was Delilah.

And the lords of the Philistines came up unto her, and said unto her, Entice him, and see wherein his great strength lieth, and by what means we may prevail against him, that we may bind him to afflict him: and we will give thee every one of us eleven hundred pieces of silver.

And Delilah said to Samson, Tell me, I pray thee, wherein thy great strength lieth, and wherewith thou mightest be bound to afflict thee . . .

And it came to pass, when she pressed him daily with her words, and urged him, so that his soul was vexed unto death;

That he told her all his heart, and said unto her, There hath not come a rasor upon mine head; for I have been a Nazarite unto

PETER PAUL RUBENS (1577–1640),
*SAMSON AND DELILAH.*

God from my mother's womb: if I be shaven, then my strength will go from me, and I shall become weak, and be like any other man.

And when Delilah saw that he had told her all his heart, she sent and called for the lords of the Philistines, saying, Come up this once, for he hath shewed me all his heart. Then the lords of the Philistines came up unto her, and brought money in their hand.

And she made him sleep upon her knees; and she called for a man, and she caused him to shave off the seven locks of his head; and she began to afflict him, and his strength went from him.

And she said, The Philistines be upon thee, Samson. And he awoke out of his sleep, and said, I will go out as at other times before, and shake myself. And he wist not that the Lord was departed from him.

But the Philistines took him, and put out his eyes, and brought him down to Gaza, and bound him with fetters of brass; and he did grind in the prison house.

Howbeit the hair of his head began to grow again after he was shaven.

Then the lords of the Philistines gathered them together for to offer a great sacrifice unto Dagon their god, and to rejoice: for they said, Our god hath delivered Samson our enemy into our hand.

And when the people saw him, they praised their god: for they said, Our god hath delivered into our hands our enemy, and the destroyer of our country, which slew many of us.

And it came to pass, when their hearts were merry, that they said, Call for Samson, that he may make us sport. And they called for Samson out of the prison house; and he made them sport: and they set him between the pillars.

And Samson said unto the lad that held him by the hand, Suffer me that I may feel the pillars whereupon the house standeth, that I may lean upon them.

Now the house was full of men and women; and all the lords of the Philistines were there; and there were upon the roof about three thousand men and women, that beheld while Samson made sport.

And Samson called unto the Lord, and said, O Lord God, remember me, I pray thee, and strengthen me, I pray thee, only this once, O God, that I may be avenged of the Philistines for my two eyes.

And Samson took hold of the two middle pillars on which the house stood, and on which it was borne up, of the one with this right hand, and of the other with his left.

And Samson said, Let me die with the Philistines. And he bowed himself with all his might, and the house fell upon the lords, and upon all the people that were therein. So the dead which he slew at his death were more than they which he slew in his life.

# The Holy Family

When [Jesus] was twelve years old, they went up to Jerusalem after the custom of the feast.

And when they had fulfilled the days, as they returned, the child Jesus tarried behind in Jerusalem; and Joseph and his mother knew not of it.

But they, supposing him to have been in the company, went a day's journey; and they sought him among their kinsfolk and acquaintance.

And when they found him not, they turned back again to Jerusalem, seeking him.

And it came to pass, that after three days they found him in the temple, sitting in the midst of the doctors, both hearing them, and asking them questions.

And all that heard him were astonished at his understanding and answers.

And when they saw him, they were amazed: and his mother said unto him, Son, why hast thou thus dealt with us? behold, thy father and I have sought thee sorrowing.

And he said unto them, How is it that ye sought me? wist ye not that I must be about my Father's business?

And they understood not the saying which he spake unto them.

And he went down with them, and came to Nazareth, and was subject unto them: but his mother kept all these sayings in her heart.

Luke chapter 2, verses 42 to 51.

WILLIAM HOLMAN HUNT (1827–1910),
THE FINDING OF THE YOUNG SAVIOUR IN
THE TEMPLE (DETAIL).

109

SIR EDWARD JOHN POYNTER (1836–1919),
*PRODIGAL'S RETURN.*

# THE PRODIGAL SON

A certain man had two sons:

And the younger of them said to his father, Father, give me the portion of goods that falleth to me. And he divided unto them his living.

And not many days after the younger son gathered all together, and took his journey into a far country, and there wasted his substance with riotous living.

And when he had spent all, there arose a mighty famine in that land; and he began to be in want.

And he went and joined himself to a citizen of that country; and he sent him into his fields to feed swine.

And he would fain have filled his belly with the husks that the swine did eat: and no man gave unto him.

And when he came to himself, he said, How many hired servants of my Father's have bread enough and to spare, and I perish with hunger!

I will arise and go to my Father, and will say unto him, Father, I have sinned against heaven, and before thee,

And am no more worthy to be called thy son: make me as one of thy hired servants.

And he arose, and came to his father. But when he was yet a great way off, his father saw him, and had compassion, and ran, and fell on his neck, and kissed him.

And the son said unto him, Father, I have sinned against heaven, and in thy sight, and am no more worthy to be called thy son.

But the father said to his servants, Bring forth the best robe, and put it on him; and put a ring on his hand, and shoes on his feet:

And bring hither the fatted calf, and kill it, and let us eat, and be merry:

For this my son was dead, and is alive again; he was lost, and is found.

# THE JUDGMENT OF SOLOMON

Then came there two women, that were harlots, unto the king, and stood before him.

And the one woman said, O my lord, I and this woman dwell in one house; and I was delivered of a child with her in the house.

And it came to pass the third day after that I was delivered, that this woman was delivered also: and we were together; there was no stranger with us in the house, save we two in the house.

And this woman's child died in the night; because she overlaid it.

And she arose at midnight, and took my son from beside me, while thine handmaid slept, and laid it in her bosom, and laid her dead child in my bosom.

And when I rose in the morning to give my child suck, behold, it was dead: but when I had considered it in the morning, behold, it was not my son, which I did bear.

And the other woman said, Nay; but the living is my son, and the dead is thy son. And this said, No; but the dead is thy son, and the living is my son. Thus they spake before the king.

Then said the king, The one saith, This is my son that liveth, and thy son is the dead: and the other saith, Nay; but thy son is the dead, and my son is the living.

And the king said, Bring me a sword. And they brought a sword before the king.

And the king said, Divide the living child in two, and give half to the one, and half to the other.

Then spake the woman whose the living child was unto the king, for her bowels yearned upon her son, and she said, O my lord, give her the living child, and in no wise slay it. But the other said, Let it be neither mine nor thine, but divide it.

Then the king answered and said, Give her the living child, and in no wise slay it: she is the mother thereof.

And all Israel heard of the judgment which the king had judged; and they feared the king: for they saw that the wisdom of God was in him, to do judgment.

I Kings chapter 3, verses 16 to 28.

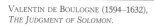

JACOPO TINTORETTO (1518–1594),
*JOSEPH AND THE WIFE OF POTIPHAR* (DETAIL).

# POTIPHAR'S WIFE

And Joseph was brought down to Egypt; and Potiphar, an officer of Pharaoh, captain of the guard, an Egyptian, bought him of the hands of the Ishmeelites, which had brought him down thither . . .

And Joseph found grace in his sight, and he served him: and he made him overseer over his house, and all that he had he put into his hand . . .

And it came to pass after these things, that his master's wife cast her eyes upon Joseph; and she said, Lie with me.

But he refused, and said unto his master's wife, Behold, my master wotteth not what is with me in the house, and he hath committed all that he hath into my hand;

There is none greater in this house than I; neither hath he kept back any thing from me but thee, because thou art his wife: how then can I do this great wickedness, and sin against God? . . .

And it came to pass about this time, that Joseph went into the house to do his business; and there was none of the men of the house there within.

And she caught him by his garment, saying, Lie with me: and he left his garment in her hand, and fled, and got him out.

And it came to pass, when she saw that he had left his garment in her hand, and was fled forth,

That she called unto the men of her house, and spake unto them, saying, See, he hath brought in an Hebrew unto us to mock us; he came in unto me to lie with me, and I cried with a loud voice:

And it came to pass, when he heard that I lifted up my voice and cried, that he left his garment with me, and fled, and got him out . . . And it came to pass, when his master heard the words of his wife, which she spake unto him, saying, After this manner did thy servant to me; that his wrath was kindled.

And Joseph's master took him, and put him into the prison, a place where the king's prisoners were bound: and he was there in the prison.

But the Lord was with Joseph, and shewed him mercy, and gave him favour in the sight of the keeper of the prison.

Genesis chapter 39, verses 1, 4, 7
to 9, 11 to 15 and 19 to 21.

115

# Ruth and Boaz

Ruth the Moabitess said unto Naomi, Let me now go to the field, and glean ears of corn . . . And she said unto her, Go, my daughter.

And she went, and came, and gleaned in the field after the reapers: and her hap was to light on a part of the field belonging unto Boaz, who was of the kindred of Elimelech.

And, behold, Boaz came from Bethlehem, and said unto the reapers, The Lord be with you. And they answered him, The Lord bless thee.

Then said Boaz unto his servant that was set over the reapers, Whose damsel is this.

And the servant that was set over the reapers answered and said, It is the Moabitish damsel . . .

And when she was risen up to glean, Boaz commanded his young men, saying, Let her glean even among the sheaves, and reproach her not:

And let fall also some of the handfuls of purpose for her, and leave them, that she may glean them, and rebuke her not . . .

And when Boaz had eaten and was drunk, and his heart was merry, he went to lie down at the end of the heap of corn: and she came softly, and uncovered his feet, and laid her down.

And it came to pass at midnight, that the man was afraid, and turned himself: and, behold, a woman lay at his feet.

And he said, Who art thou? And she answered, I am Ruth, thine handmaid . . . And she lay at his feet until the morning.

So Boaz took Ruth, and she was his wife: and when he went in unto her, the Lord gave her conception, and she bare a son.

Ruth chapter 2, verses 2 to 6 and 15 to 16, chapter 3, verses 7 to 9 and 14, and chapter 4, verse 13.

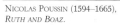

JAN VERMEER (1632–1675),
*CHRIST IN THE HOUSE OF MARY AND MARTHA.*

# MARY AND MARTHA

Now it came to pass, as they went, that he entered into a certain village: and a certain woman named Martha received him into her house.

And she had a sister called Mary, which also sat at Jesus' feet, and heard his word.

But Martha was cumbered about much serving, and came to him, and said, Lord, dost thou not care that my sister hath left me to serve alone? bid her therefore that she help me.

And Jesus answered and said unto her, Martha, Martha, thou art careful and troubled about many things:

But one thing is needful: and Mary hath chosen that good part, which shall not be taken away from her.

# DAVID AND BATHSHEBA

David sent Joab, and his servants with him, and all Israel; and they destroyed the children of Ammon, and besieged Rabbah. But David tarried still at Jerusalem.

And it came to pass in an eveningtide, that David arose from off his bed, and walked upon the roof of the king's house: and from the roof he saw a woman washing herself; and the woman was very beautiful to look upon.

And David sent and inquired after the woman. And one said, Is not this Bathsheba, the daughter of Eliam, the wife of Uriah the Hittite?

And David sent messengers, and took her; and she came in unto him, and he lay with her; for she was purified from her uncleanness: and she returned unto her house.

And the woman conceived, and sent and told David, and said, I am with child . . .

And it came to pass in the morning that David wrote a letter to Joab, and sent it by the hand of Uriah.

And he wrote in the letter, saying, Set ye Uriah in the forefront of the hottest battle, and retire ye from him, that he may be smitten, and die.

And it came to pass, when Joab observed the city, that he assigned Uriah unto a place where he knew the valiant men were.

And the men of the city went out, and fought with Joab: and there fell some of the people of the servants of David; and Uriah the Hittite died also . . .

And when the wife of Uriah heard that Uriah her husband was dead, she mourned for her husband.

And when the mourning was past, David sent and fetched her to his house, and she became his wife, and bare him a son. But the thing that David had done displeased the Lord.

PETER PAUL RUBENS (1577–1640),
*BATHSHEBA RECEIVING DAVID'S LETTER.*

121

RAPHAEL (1483–1520),
*CHRIST'S CHARGE TO ST PETER.*

# LOYALTY AND TRUST

When they had dined, Jesus saith to Simon Peter, Simon, son of Jonas, lovest thou me more than these? He saith unto him, Yea, Lord; thou knowest that I love thee. He saith unto him, Feed my lambs.

He saith to him again the second time, Simon, son of Jonas, lovest thou me? He saith unto him, Yea, Lord, thou knowest that I love thee. He saith unto him, Feed my sheep.

He saith unto him the third time, Simon, son of Jonas, lovest thou me? Peter was grieved because he said unto him the third time, Lovest thou me? And he said unto him, Lord, thou knowest all things; thou knowest that I love thee. Jesus saith unto him, Feed my sheep.

# Turn the Other Cheek

Ye have heard that it hath been said, An eye for an eye, and a tooth for a tooth:

But I say unto you, That ye resist not evil: but whosoever shall smite thee on the right cheek, turn to him the other also . . .

Ye have heard that it hath been said, Thou shalt love thy neighbour, and hate thine enemy.

But I say unto you, Love your enemies, bless them that curse you, do good to them that hate you, and pray for them which despitefully use you, and persecute you;

That ye may be the children of your father which is in heaven: for he maketh his sun to rise on the evil and on the good, and sendeth rain on the just and on the unjust.

For if ye love them which love you, what reward have ye? do not even the publicans the same?

And if ye salute your brethren only, what do ye more than others? do not even the publicans so?

Be ye therefore perfect, even as your Father which is in heaven is perfect.

Matthew chapter 5, verses 38 to 39 and 43 to 48.

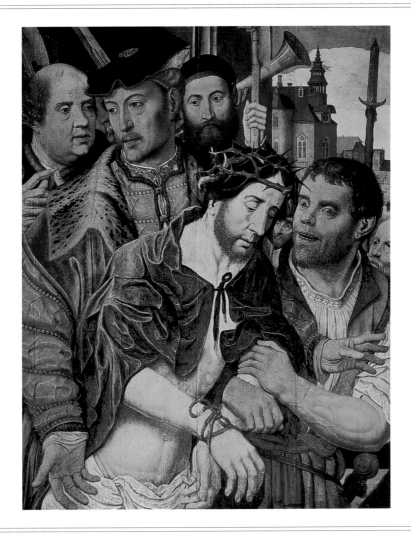

JAN MOSTAERT (C.1475–C.1555),
ECCE HOMO

# Suggested Reading for Each Sunday of the Christian year

| | |
|---|---|
| 9th Sunday before Christmas: | The good Samaritan. p.59 |
| 8th Sunday before Christmas: | A woman caught committing adultery. p.55 |
| 7th Sunday before Christmas: | Jacob's dream. p.67 |
| 6th Sunday before Christmas: | The Sheep and the Goats. p.103 |
| 5th Sunday before Christmas: | David and Goliath. p.95 |
| Advent Sunday: | The Beatitudes. p.60 |
| Advent 2: | The heavenly Jerusalem. p.68 |
| Advent 3: | Job's faith. p.91 |
| Advent 4: | The annunciation to the shepherds. p.56 |
| Sunday after Christmas Day: | Isaiah preaches comfort. p.47 |
| 2nd Sunday after Christmas: | God as a shepherd. p.52 |
| Epiphany 1: | The Magi. p.83 |
| * Epiphany 2: | The slaughter of the innocents. p.28 |
| Epiphany 3: | Isaiah on the saviour of the world. p.51 |
| Epiphany 4: | The Holy Family. p.108 |
| Epiphany 5: | The power of evil broken. p.48 |
| Epiphany 6: | A sinful woman weeps beside Jesus. p.31 |
| 9th Sunday before Easter: | Peter denies his friendship with Jesus. p.35 |
| 8th Sunday before Easter: | Loyalty and trust. p.123 |
| 7th Sunday before Easter: | Turn the other cheek. p.124 |
| Lent 1: | The suffering servant. p.24 |
| Lent 2: | Job. p.23 |
| Lent 3: | Isaiah's vision in the Temple. p.76 |
| Lent 4: | The Annunciation. p.79 |
| Lent 5: | Jeremiah, punished and comforted. p.64 |
| Palm Sunday: | A ram caught in a thicket. p.80 |
| Easter Day: | Mary Magdalen at the tomb of Jesus. p.40 |
| Easter 1: | Doubting Thomas. p.75 |

* In some years there may be fewer Sundays between Epiphany and Lent, and more Sundays between Pentecost and Advent.